A Robbie Reader

What's So Great About . . . ?

FRANCIS SCOTT KEY

Marylou Morano Kjelle

P.O. Box 196
Hockessin, Delaware 19707
Visit us on the web: www.mitchelllane.com
Comments? email us: mitchelllane@mitchelllane.com

Printing 1 2 3 4 5 6 7 8 9

A Robbie Reader/What's So Great About . . . ?

Annie Oakley
Daniel Boone
Davy Crockett
Ferdinand Magellan
Francis Scott Key
Henry Hudson
Jacques Cartier
Johnny Appleseed
Robert Fulton
Sam Houston

Library of Congress Cataloging-in-Publication Data
Kjelle, Marylou Morano.
Francis Scott Key / by Marylou Morano Kjelle.
p. cm. — (A Robbie Reader. What's so great about—?)
Includes bibliographical references and index.
ISBN 1-58415-474-8 (library bound : alk. paper)
1. Key, Francis Scott, 1779–1843—Juvenile literature. 2. Poets, American—19th century—Biography—Juvenile literature. 3. United States—History—War of 1812—Biography—Juvenile literature. 4. Patriotic poetry, American—Authorship—Juvenile literature. 5. Star-spangled banner (Song)—Juvenile literature. I. Title. II. Series.
PS2168.K57 2006
811'.2—dc22
[B] 2005028508

ISBN-10: 1-58415-474-8 ISBN 13: 978-1-58415-474-7

ABOUT THE AUTHOR: Marylou Morano Kjelle is a freelance writer and photojournalist who lives and works in central New Jersey. She is a regular contributor to several local newspaper and online publications. She has written over 20 nonfiction books for young readers, including *Hilary Duff* and *Tony Hawk* for Mitchell Lane Publishers. Marylou has a master's of science degree from Rutgers University. She teaches English and writing at Rutgers and several other colleges in New Jersey.

PHOTO CREDITS: Cover, pp. 1, 4, 6, 14, 22, 24, 25—Library of Congress; pp. 7, 12, 18, 21—Sharon Beck; p. 8—Barbara Marvis; p. 10—Hulton Archive/Getty Images; p. 16—Anapolis & Anne Arundel County.; p. 26—Yogi, Inc./CORBIS.

PLB

TABLE OF CONTENTS

Words in **bold** type can be found in the glossary.

In Percy Moran's portrait *The Star-Spangled Banner,* Francis Scott Key peers across the Chesapeake Bay to see whether the American flag is still flying over Fort McHenry. The sight of the still-waving flag inspired Key to write the poem for "The Star-Spangled Banner."

Victory!

It was early on the morning of September 14, 1814. The sun was rising over the Chesapeake (CHEH-sah-peek) Bay. Francis Scott Key, a lawyer from Maryland, peered hopefully into the fog and mist. He wanted to see whether the American flag was still flying over Fort McHenry.

For many hours, American and British soldiers had battled for the fort, which was at the entrance to Baltimore (BALL-tih-moor) Harbor. The two countries were fighting a war that had started in 1812. The British had already destroyed the new American capital, Washington, D.C. Now they wanted to destroy Baltimore. To get there, they first had to capture Fort McHenry.

During the battle of Fort McHenry, rockets and bombs burst in the air as the British tried to take the fort. Key wrote of these things in "The Star-Spangled Banner."

A few days before the attack on the fort, Key had sailed under a flag of **truce** to the British **flagship.** He had asked the vice admiral to release his friend, Dr. William Beanes, an American who had been captured by the British. Now the British soldiers were holding both men on a small boat at sea.

Throughout the long night, Key watched the battle from the deck of the boat. He saw bombs and rockets soar through the darkness. Some burst in the air and lit up the sky with a

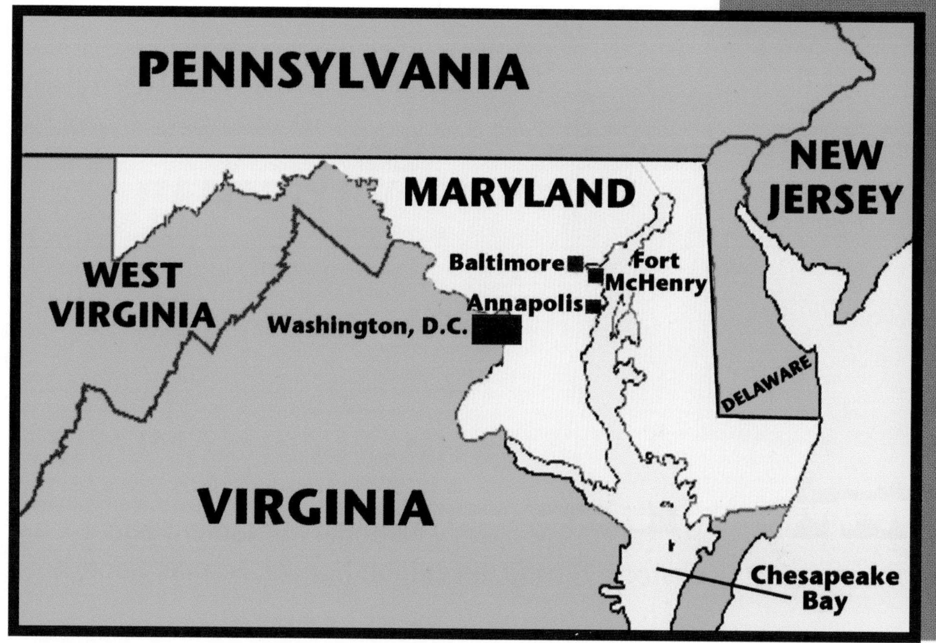

Fort McHenry was built during the Revolutionary War to protect Baltimore from attack by the British. It is surrounded on three sides by water, so an enemy ship that wished to enter Baltimore Harbor first had to pass by the fort. It was named after James McHenry, the first Secretary of War.

red glare. Key wondered if Fort McHenry could hold up. It helped to know that those guarding the fort had expected the attack. They had prepared the fort with **ramparts** and sandbags.

As morning approached, the fighting stopped. Who had won the battle? When dawn broke with early light, Key saw that "our flag was still there." The fort had not fallen. Baltimore was safe.

At the Fort McHenry National Monument and Historic Shrine, an exhibit honors Francis Scott Key.

Key was a poet as well as a lawyer. He was proud of the American victory, and he wanted all Americans to know how he felt. “My heart spoke,” is how he explained it.

Key began to write a poem about the American flag. It began with the words:

> *Oh, say can you see, by the dawn’s*
> *early light . . .*

Today every American knows these words by heart. Citizens sing them at official events and before sports games. Key’s words became the country’s national **anthem**.

Defence of Fort M'Henry

O ! say can you see by the dawn's early light,
What so proudly we hailed at the twilight's last gleaming,
Whose broad stripes and bright stars through the perilous fight,
O'er the ramparts we watch'd, were so gallantly streaming?
And the Rockets' red glare, the Bombs bursting in air,
Gave proof through the night that our Flag was still there;

O ! say does that star-spangled Banner yet wave,
O'er the Land of the free, and the home of the brave?

On the shore dimly seen through the mists of the deep,
Where the foe's haughty host in dread silence reposes,
What is that which the breeze, o'er the towering steep,
As it fitfully blows, half conceals, half discloses?
Now it catches the gleam of the morning's first beam,
In full glory reflected new shines in the stream,

'Tis the star-spangled banner, O ! long may it wave
O'er the land of the free and the home of the brave.

And where is that band who so vauntingly swore
That the havoc of war and the battle's confusion,
A home and a country, shall leave us no more?
Their blood has washed out their foul footsteps pollution.
No refuge could save the hireling and slave,
From the terror of flight or the gloom of the grave,

And the star-spangled banner in triumph doth wave,
O'er the Land of the Free, and the Home of the Brave.

O ! thus be it ever when freemen shall stand,
Between their lov'd home, and the war's desolation,
Blest with vict'ry and peace, may the Heav'n rescued land,
Praise the Power that hath made and preserv'd us a nation!
Then conquer we must, when our cause it is just,
And this be our motto—"In God is our Trust;"

And the star-spangled Banner in triumph shall wave,
O'er the Land of the Free, and the Home of the Brave.

Most Americans can sing the first stanza of "The Star-Spangled Banner" from memory, but there are three more stanzas to the song. When the poem was first distributed, it was called "Defence of Fort M'Henry."

The love of country developed by Young Frankie (above) may have come from his father. Mr. Key fought in the Revolutionary War, and he often told his son about it. He also taught Young Frankie how to shoot a gun.

Young Frankie

Francis Scott Key was born on August 1, 1779, in Carroll County, Maryland. His nickname was Young Frankie.

Francis's father, John Ross Key, fought in the Revolutionary War. Later, Mr. Key became a lawyer and a judge. Francis's mother was Ann Phoebe Penn. The Keys lived on a **plantation** called Terra Rubra. Like many plantation owners in those times, they had slaves. Mrs. Key taught their slaves how to read and write.

Francis had one sister named Ann. Ann and Francis lived in a happy home. Terra Rubra was in a valley of the Blue Ridge Mountains. For fun, Francis and Ann explored the meadows around their home. When he was much older,

An aerial view of Annapolis in winter. Construction on the main part of the Maryland State House, in the center of the circle, began in 1772 and was completed in 1779, the year Key was born. Work was still being done on the dome's interior when Key went to live with his grandmother in 1789.

Francis wrote a poem for Ann about those days. He wrote:

> Those sunny paths were all our own,
> And you and I were there alone.

Mrs. Key taught Francis how to read before he was six years old. She sang him songs and told him stories. Mr. Key took Francis fishing. He taught him how to ride a horse and shoot a gun.

Francis and Ann often visited the city of Annapolis with their parents. Annapolis was the capital of Maryland. Many important **politicians** lived there, including at least four of the signers of the Declaration of Independence.

When he was ten years old, Francis went to live with his father's mother, Ann Arnold Key, in Annapolis. Francis loved Grandmother Key, who was blind. From that point on, Francis spent long periods of time away from home—but he returned to his beloved Terra Rubra as often as he could.

A portrait of Key made around the time he wrote "The Star-Spangled Banner." His poem made Americans look at their flag with pride. It

F. S. Key

In Annapolis, Francis Scott Key went to a **preparatory school**, then to St. John's College. He graduated from the college in 1796.

Key was a **Christian** of deep faith. He thought about becoming a minister. His father's brother, Philip Barton Key, thought the boy would make a good lawyer. After graduation, Francis lived with his uncle Philip in Annapolis while he studied law.

When he was eighteen years old, Francis met Mary Tayloe Lloyd, the granddaughter of a **royal governor.** On January 19, 1802, they were married. Francis and Mary moved to an area of Maryland near Washington, D.C., called

St. John's College in Annapolis was founded in 1696 as King William's School. It is the third oldest college in America. Key graduated from the school in its 100th year.

Georgetown. Mary was a good hostess, and the Key home was often full of friends.

Francis and his uncle Philip became law partners. By the time he was twenty-eight years old, Francis was a well-known lawyer. He went by the name of F.S. Key.

Key treated his clients fairly. He provided legal services at no charge for anyone who had fought in the Revolutionary War. He also did not charge former slaves or poor people. He stood to his full six feet as he argued their cases in court. It was said of him that he spoke as though "lightning charg[ed] his sentences with electrical power."

Francis and Mary had eleven children—six sons and five daughters. Key was a good father who enjoyed spending time with his family. He gave his children a love of books and music.

Although he was a busy father and lawyer, Key often had time to write poetry. He wrote little poems for his family that he would leave here and there for them to find. He also wrote **hymns**. Some are still sung in the **Episcopalian** Church.

Many of the battles in the War of 1812 took place near Canada, Washington, D.C., and the Gulf of Mexico, a large body of water to the south of the United States. Many battles were also fought at sea.

After the Battle

After the victory at Fort McHenry, the British freed Key and Dr. Beanes. As they sailed back to Baltimore, Key continued to work on his poem. When he was finished, the poem had four **stanzas**.

The day after he returned, Key showed his poem to his brother-in-law, Judge Joseph H. Nicholson. Nicholson had been a commander at Fort McHenry. The poem had no title, so Nicholson called it "Defence of Fort M'Henry."

The poem was first printed on **handbills.** Then it appeared in newspapers. Soon almost everyone in Baltimore had a copy, but no one knew it had been written by Key. All the public knew was that it had been written by "a gentleman of Maryland."

A popular song at the time was "To Anacreon in Heaven." It was written by John Stafford Smith and first sung in England around 1780. Legend has it that Key had "To Anacreon in Heaven" in mind when he wrote his poem, because the words fit its melody. Now not only were people reciting "Defence of Fort M'Henry," they were also singing it. By then Key had a new name for his song. He called it "The Star-Spangled Banner."

On December 24, 1814, the War of 1812 ended. Life began to return to the way it was before the war. One of the most important issues of the day was the question of slavery. Key was against slavery. He called it the "wickedness of man." Yet he owned slaves. Many people did not understand this **contradiction**.

But Key knew that life was not easy for many former slaves. He wanted to give freed slaves, and blacks who had been born free, the chance to return to Africa. Other Americans thought that free blacks would cause trouble. They wanted them out of the country.

Key and a few other white men formed the American Colonization Society. This group founded a colony in Africa where freed slaves could live. The colony was named Liberia. It became a **republic** of Africa in 1847.

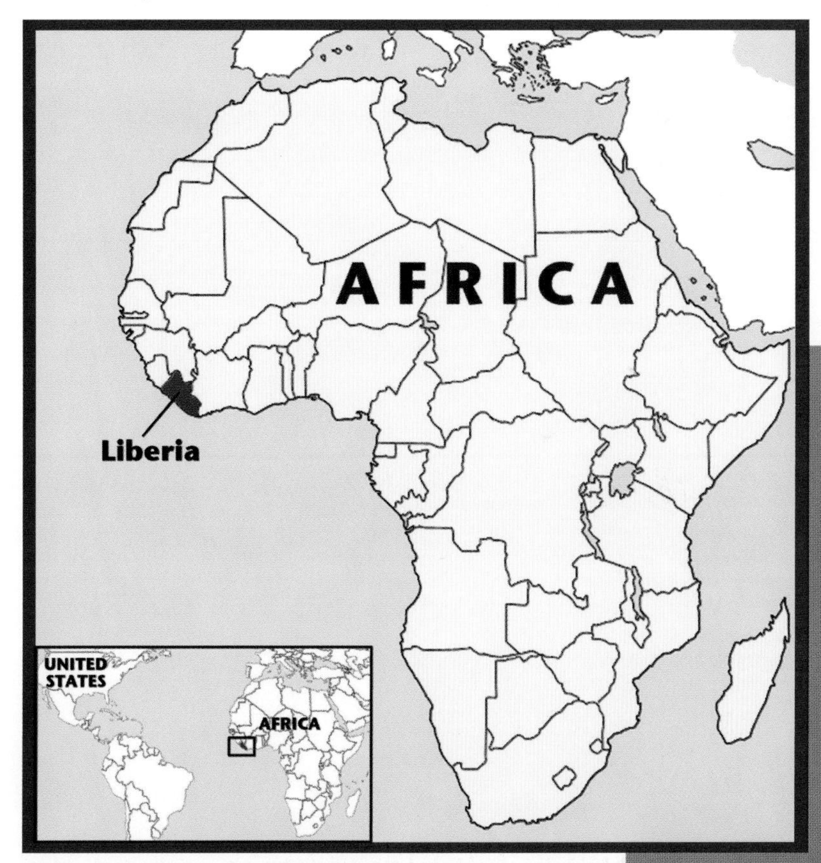

Key and others wanted Liberia to be a place where those who had been slaves could truly be free. The first ship left for Liberia in 1820 with 88 black colonists. Many died of disease a few weeks after arriving in Liberia.

ey and his family lived in the Key Mansion on M Street in Georgetow
section of Washington, D.C. When a highway was built in the area i
948, the Keys' house was taken apart and the pieces stored. Th
ieces were stolen and the house was never put back together agai

Last Years

One of Key's friends was President Andrew Jackson. In 1833, President Jackson asked Key to go to Alabama. Pioneers had settled on land that belonged to the Creek Indians. The pioneers refused to leave, and riots had broken out. Key went to Alabama and drew up a plan under which they all could live in peace.

That same year, President Jackson made Key district attorney of Washington, D.C. As district attorney, he was the official lawyer for the capital city. Key worked as district attorney until 1841.

In January of 1843, Key caught a cold while visiting Baltimore. The cold turned to

CHAPTER FIVE

Andrew Jackson fought in the War of 1812 and helped defeat the British in the Battle of New Orleans. In 1824 he became the seventh president of the United States. As president, he trusted his friend F. S. Key with important matters. One of those was making peace between the settlers and the Creek Indians in Alabama.

pneumonia (noo-MOH-nyah), and he died on January 11. He was buried at Mount Olivet Cemetery in Frederick, Maryland. His gravesite is one of just a few places allowed to fly the American flag both day and night.

The American flag that inspired Francis Scott Key to write "The Star-Spangled Banner" is now at the Smithsonian Institution in Washington, D.C. The oldest copy of the poem written in Key's handwriting is at the Maryland Historical Society in Baltimore.

The Smithsonian Institution in Washington, D.C., is actually a collection of national museums. All the museums together house more than three million items, including the flag that had flown over Fort McHenry and inspired Key to write his famous poem.

In 1931, Congress voted to make "The Star-Spangled Banner" the national anthem of the United States. President Herbert Hoover made it a law that year on March 3.

Key had a deep love of God, family, and country, and he made his mark in history in many ways. He was a good lawyer who treated people fairly. He worked hard doing what he thought would make life better for slaves. He helped keep the peace between Native Americans and settlers. But it is for "The Star-Spangled Banner" that he is most remembered.

The Key Monument in Mount Olivet Cemetery in Frederick, Maryland, where Key is buried. Monuments have been erected in memory of Francis Scott Key in Maryland and in California.

CHRONOLOGY

1779 Francis Scott Key is born on August 1.

1789 Francis goes to live with his grandmother in Annapolis.

1796 Francis graduates from St. John's College in Annapolis.

1802 Francis marries Mary Tayloe Lloyd. They will have 11 children.

1812 The United States declares war on Britain, and the War of 1812 begins on June 18.

1814 Key begins writing "The Star-Spangled Banner" on September 14. The War of 1812 ends later that year.

1816 Key and other men form the American Colonization Society.

1833 Key goes to Alabama to settle a land dispute between settlers and the Creek Indians. He becomes district attorney for Washington, D.C.

1843 Francis Scott Key dies on January 11.

1931 President Herbert Hoover approves making "The Star-Spangled Banner" the national anthem of the United States.

TIMELINE IN HISTORY

1754 The French and Indian War begins in North America.

1770 The Boston Massacre occurs on March 5 when a group of British soldiers stationed in Boston fires into a crowd of angry citizens.

1773 The Boston Tea Party occurs on December 16 when Boston citizens throw 342 chests of tea into Boston Harbor.

1774 The First Continental Congress meets from September 5 to October 26.

1775 The battles of Lexington and Concord are fought on April 19, officially starting the Revolutionary War.

1776 The Declaration of Independence is signed.

1777 Betsy Ross's flag is adopted as the official flag of the United States.

1783 The Revolutionary War officially comes to an end when the Treaty of Paris is signed on September 3.

1788 Maryland becomes the seventh state to ratify the U.S. Constitution.

1789 George Washington becomes the first president of the United States.

1800 The second American president, John Adams, and his wife, Abigail, move into a partially finished White House.

1807	Robert Fulton is the first to use a steam engine to power a boat.
1812	The British invade the United States, beginning the War of 1812.
1814	Washington, D.C., is burned by the British.
1845	Annapolis, Maryland, becomes the site of the United States Naval Academy.
1860	Abraham Lincoln is elected president.
1861	The Confederates fire against Fort Sumter, and the Civil War begins.

FIND OUT MORE

Books

Bowdish, Lynea. *Francis Scott Key and "The Star-Spangled Banner."* New York: Mondo Publishing, 2002.

Gregson, Susan R. *Francis Scott Key: Patriotic Poet.* Mankato, Minneapolis: Bridgestone Books, 2003.

Kroll, Steven. *By the Dawn's Early Light.* New York: Scholastic, Inc., 2000.

Quiri, Patricia Ryon. *The National Anthem.* New York: Children's Press, 1998.

Works Consulted

Benn, Carl. *The War of 1812.* New York, Routledge, 2003.

Filby, P.W. *Star Spangled Books.* Baltimore: Maryland Historical Society, 1972.
Hart, William J. *Stories of Our National Songs.* Boston: W.A. Wilde Company, 1942.
Key-Smith, Francis. *Francis Scott Key.* Washington: Key-Smith and Company, 1911.
Molotsky, Irvin. *The Flag, the Poet & the Song.* New York: Dutton. 2001.
Muller, Charles, G. *The Darkest Day: The Washington-Baltimore Campaign During the War of 1812.* Philadelphia: University of Pennsylvania Press, 2003.
Swanson, Neil H. *The Perilous Fight.* New York: Farrar and Rinehart, 1945.
Weybright, Victor. *Spangled Banner.* New York: Farrar and Rinehart, Inc., 1935.

On the Internet

The Flag of the United States of America, "Francis Scott Key"
http://www.usflag.org/history/francisscottkey.html
Fort McHenry: Birthplace of Our National Anthem
http://www.bcpl.net/~etowner/anthem.html
Virtual Museum of History: "Francis Scott Key" (with research links)
http://www.francisscottkey.org/

GLOSSARY

anthem (AN-thum)—A song of praise.

Christian (KRIS-chin)—One who follows Jesus Christ.

contradiction (kon-truh-DIK-shun)—A statement that seems to say two opposite things.

Episcopalian (ee-PIS-kuh-pay-lee-un)—A branch of the Christian religion.

flagship (FLAG-ship)—The head ship in a fleet; the one that carries the commander.

handbill (HAND-bill)—A small sheet of paper that is given out to the public.

hymn (HIM)—A religious song.

plantation (plan-TAY-shun)—A large farm.

politician (pah-lih-TIH-shun)—A person involved in governing.

preparatory school (preh-PAH-ruh-tor-ee skool)—A school that prepares students for college.

ramparts (RAM-parts)—Strong walls that are built around a fort.

republic (ree-PUB-lik)—A system of government that has a president and citizens who have the right to vote.

royal governor (ROY-ul GUH-ver-nur)—A governor appointed by the king.

stanza (STAN-za)—Several lines in a poem that go together.

truce (TROOS)—An agreement to stop a war.

INDEX